Word to My Kings & Queens

Achieving a Renewed & Improved Mind

MARVIN "MERV" MATTAIR

AMANI PUBLISHING
BARBARA JOE-WILLIAMS

Published by:

Amani Publishing
P. O. Box 12045
Tallahassee, FL 32317
www.AmaniPublishing.net
850-264-3341

A company based on faith, hope, and love

ISBN-13: 9780978893774

ISBN-10: 0978893778

LCCN: 2007938110

Cover photograph courtesy of: *Istockphoto.com*

Author's photograph by: *Glenda_Branch@yahoo.com*

Dedication

This book is dedicated to all of the "Small Town Heroes" that play an important role in the shaping of a young person's life. If you are a father who's doing what is expected of you, then you are a hero who's making a positive impact on your child and other children.

If you are a mother doing what is expected of you, then you are a hero. If you are a teacher who's teaching to the best of your abilities, then you are indeed a hero. If you are a preacher who's spreading the gospel and living up to what you preach, you are a hero.

If you are a bus driver who's taking pride in getting children home safely to their parents, you are a hero. If you are a janitor who's holding young people accountable even though its not in your job description, you are a hero. If you are homeless but every chance you get, you say something positive to a young person, you are a hero. If you are a soldier in the military who went to war for the betterment of our children's future, you are a hero.

If you are a coach who spends time with young people, you are a hero. If you are a cook in the kitchen of a school that takes pride in feeding young people, you are a hero. If you work with juveniles at some sort of facility and take pride in rehabilitating them, you are a hero.

If you are a grandparent, auntie, uncle, friend, step parent, cousin, sibling, who's taking care of someone else's child and raising them like they're your own, then you are a hero.

And if you love and treat everyone the same no matter what race they are, you are indeed a hero that's breaking trends.

Every "Small Town Hero" of Madison, Florida, and all other places, hold your heads up because even though you struggle, you sweat, you bleed, you suffer, you are making a world of difference in some young person's life; therefore, it gives me pleasure to say that wearing a cape doesn't signify you being a hero, your contributions to this world and to our young people is enough alone.

I don't mind telling you that I love you all, and I thank you so very much.

May God bless you all.

Marvin "Merv" Mattair
Author

Table of Contents

Introduction

Before you read this book, I would like for you to pray that you will get something from reading it because it is indeed packed with valuable information. I don't intend for anyone to follow in my footsteps, but I do expect the reader to learn from some of my mistakes and make your life a success. I have always tried my best and will continue to spread positive information through counseling sessions, public speaking, motivational speaking, etc., but I have yet to reach my number of desired people, so I was blessed with the idea of putting my words in the form of a book entitled, *Word to My Kings & Queens: Achieving a Renewed & Improved Mind.*

This book is intended to encourage every young man and every young woman who struggles with fitting in with their group of peers or struggles with breaking out from their group of peers; the ones who have made mistakes in their lives and feel that there is no way out; the ones who don't believe in the power of God; and the ones who have let the ways of this world take their focus off of the more important things in their lives. I struggled as a young man by making decisions that were more to please my peers and not my parents and there were consequences. This is why I want you to really read my story critically.

This book is also intended for all adults who struggle in marriages, struggle with responsibilities, and the ones who are strongly affected by the ways of this world. I have witnessed a great deal of marriages deteriorate and it bothers me because our children are the main ones suffering through it all. I feel that we, as adults, have to set the tone for our children by living and loving the right way no matter what the circumstances are. It's our responsibility to teach them how to be kings and queens.

Marvin "Merv" Mattair - 6

Chapter 1

From a Boy to a King

INTRODUCTION: This section of my book is geared towards opening the eyes of young individuals who are living for the moment and not worrying about the future. The ones who are being impulsive and not thinking before responding and being a follower of what's wrong instead of being a leader of what's right.

INTENTION: My intention is to get you to realize that you are going to make mistakes and sometimes fall on this journey, but you are not counted out unless you stay on the ground. I want you to know that you are unique in several ways and nobody can do what you do the way that you do it. I want you to realize that being hard and negative will eventually lead you in the arms of the law if you don't decide to make changes in the way that you carry yourself. I don't want you to give up on your dreams no matter what happens to you on this journey, just adjust to the situation and fight to the end. You are royalty!

When I was attending high school in 1993, I was young, cocky, and head strong. I wanted to challenge everything and everybody. I did not want to be corrected nor did I show sympathy for victims of my verbal abuse or physical abuse. I thought that it was a must to please and impress my so called "homeboys" by cursing around them, sagging my pants, and disrespecting young ladies.

My mom and dad had always told me that it only takes a second to get in trouble, but it sometimes takes years to get out of it. I can say that I was blessed to have my real mom and real dad to raise me and that they did a real good job. They taught me and all of my brothers and sisters the correct way to act in public so if we strayed away from what they had taught us, it was because of peer pressure or curiosity. I wanted to fit in, so I guess you can say that I was down for whatever. I did not mind fighting because I did not have any fear in my heart. I would use all kinds of nasty words because a lot of the rappers used them and people still gave them respect so I expected the same results. I shortly realized that there was a price to pay for being down for whatever and a follower of negative people, such as having enemies, not being respected by teachers, receiving failing grades, being labeled bad, etc. I did not care about all of this because I always had older women coming on to me and telling me that I was handsome and that made me feel like a man. I had older guys that I witnessed mistreat women and neglect their infants, so I went through my first year of high school thinking that it was all about me. Every opportunity I got, I was trying to be with some different girl and playing on the football team made that easy.

A lot of my friends and I viewed sex as a hobby in which the young lady would always get the bad end of the deal by being talked about. I knew better, but the majority of my time was spent around my peers. It was hard to be different because that would have made me feel abnormal, and I wanted to feel normal. I was fresh meat, as they used to call it when you first enter into the ninth grade of high school, so the other students higher than me expected to see me act a fool. I was attending school everyday with a negative attitude and a unit on my face just to show others that I was not a punk and because of that attitude, several guys wanted to try me.

I got in fights because I wanted to be hard, I had a lot of enemies because I wanted to be hard, and I did badly in school because I wanted to be hard. I felt that nothing could stop me until one day I was doing some yard work for my parents in the middle of the day. That's when a car pulled up slowly and someone rolled down the back window a little bit and pointed a gun at me while riding by. I could not run or scream for help because it came upon me very quickly and unexpected, so I was in a frozen state.

I remembered getting into it with some guys in my town a couple days before that, but I did not expect them to try and get back at me like that. I did not take that too well, but I was embarrassed to tell my friends about it because I was a leader, and I did not think that it could happen to me. I was only fifteen-years-old, but I had to suffer the consequences for my actions. I saw my life flash before my eyes, and I quickly realized that it was not worth dying over so I told my parents about it, and we telephoned the authorities.

We got to the bottom of it shortly after that, and I slowed down with my negative ways. I finished that year of school with barely passing grades, and I had to spend the majority of my summer going to summer school. I realized that if I would have just gotten my work earlier in the year, then I could have spent my summer how I wanted.

The peers that I abused verbally and physically were not seen in summer school. The peers that I laughed at when they had on a pair of old dirty shoes were not seen in summer school. The peers that did not have all of the girls and the popularity were not seen in summer school. All I saw that summer were the coolest boys and girls of that school year who had wasted their time just like me, worrying about the new shoes, clothes, and how they appealed to the viewer. The funny thing about it is that when summer school started, the shoes and clothes that we praised throughout that year were out of style and something new was on the market. I knew that I was better than that because I had two good, hard working parents who were very supportive of me and who expected better from me. So I decided to do things a little different in the way that I walked, talked, and acted from then on.

During that summer, I started going to church at Morningstar Missionary Baptist church in Madison, Florida. While there, my grandmother, Catherine Murphy, would always tell me to pray, read the Bible, and come to church. I could not understand the Bible, and I did not understand the reason for going to church when a lot of the church-going people who I knew were struggling financially, struggling to leave the ways of this world alone, and struggling at loving their neighbors.

All of that made church very boring and not worth attending, so I did not have a real interest in going. On the other hand, I prayed daily for a change to come over me in the areas of respecting people more, respecting myself more, taking my work seriously, and having a girlfriend that I could just be friends with, instead of playing games with. I started to feel good every time I finished a prayer so that encouraged me to continue praying. No, I can admit that I was not completely changed, but I was prepared to go into my tenth grade year with the intentions of having better grades and not going to summer school at the end of the school term.

When I started the tenth grade, I decided that I was going to wear jean shorts and white T-shirts for a little while to keep the attention off of me. I was so hooked on how I looked the previous year and what name brand clothes I had on that I missed the purpose of school. What I attempted to do worked for a little while, so I tried several more techniques to keep me focused such as talking less, taking different routes to my classes instead of passing by the same old crowd, respecting my teachers more, etc.

It was going pretty good except for the fact that I was not with the young lady that I felt I was supposed to be with. I was talking to different females along the way trying to find a friend that I could spend time with instead of hanging with the people who I normally got in trouble with. I did not have the desire to see a female hurt anymore. Given the fact that I have two sis' mother and a father that leads by example, I just desi' young lady better than the average girl was bein'

Word to My Kings & Queen

I noticed my prayers, slowly but surely, being answered so I continued to pray towards heaven. Trying to make relationships work that were not ordained to work, quickly tired me out to the point that I was about to give up in that area until I met a young lady in the ninth grade by the name of Denise. We kicked it for a while as friends, laughing together, and having fun with one another until we decided to make it official.

My tenth grade year was beginning to get better and better by the day. (You know how it is when you can't wait to get home to call that special person and hear their voice or be able to stop by their house and talk to them.) Things were going good because the friends that I used to get in trouble with, I broke away from and started to talk with people who could do me some good, whether they were cool or not.

I supported Denise with all of her work because she was in the ninth grade and I was in the tenth, and if I needed her help in some area, she was there for me. I was not sure that she was the friend for me until one day we were sitting outside of her mother's house, and she stated to me, "I have been praying for a young man that I can be friends with that would respect me."

I flipped out when she said that because that was the very same thing that I was looking for, just in the form of a female. I could not believe it, but I accepted it as confirmation from the Lord and went on with my life. We tried our best to make the relationship work, but it seemed to get harder and harder everyday. I struggled with my football friends calling me whipped, laughing at me when she called upon me and I depart from them, and other girls trying to talk with me in a flirting way. I struggled with some of my family members saying that she was not the one for me and some of her family members telling her the same thing. She struggled with the very same things, except her friends encouraged her to spend time with me instead of with them. I did not know what the future had in store for us because we were still young and had no clue about real love. All I know is that she kept me out of a ton of trouble and we were like the best of friends. It was a challenge for the both of us, but through the grace of the Lord, we made it through that year.

We had a good summer and it was time for her to go to the tenth grade, and I was to go to the eleventh. We were ready to get the good grades and continue to help one another out. We started out good because I was playing football, and she was a cheerleader. We had it all planned out each day on where we were going to meet each other, whether it was at her locker or my locker. We were happy every time we turned the corner and saw each other's smile, to the point that we could not help but smile back.

I was finally doing positive things consistently at school and in my community, such as helping elderly people across the street, saying "yes sir" and "yes ma'am" to every adult, motivating my peers and younger students through conversations and my actions, and respecting all females for the queens that they were.

We were not sexually active with one another because I respected her for who she was, and she respected me likewise, but as that year went on and we started to get a little older and anxious, we became sexually active. We were doing a great job at respecting one another's temple, and I feel that we could have gone a lot longer because of how our parents had raised us, but living in a small town that did not have much of anything for a young person to do on the weekends, only led to smoking, drinking, and sexual involvements.

Although I started to feel like a man, I was not prepared to hear that my friend was pregnant with my baby. I "freaked" out to the point that I cried because I felt that I had messed her life up for good.

Once her coach found out, she had to quit the cheerleading squad and be inactive in all school activities. We had not expected it to turn out like that, but we had to except it and be accountable by telling our parents and excepting the consequences. Our parents did not take it too well. They agreed on supporting us verbally but not physically. Man, I thought that I was just a "no good boy" that had just screwed up somebody's life. She had to leave the main campus and attend the Project Hope building that sat behind the school.

Denise was only sixteen, and I was seventeen years of age with a baby on the way. We made it through that year with her being pregnant, but the summer was a serious challenge. I did not know that a female could get attitudes when they become pregnant, and man, she really had one. We spent the first part of the summer together, and I was ready to throw in the towel because I felt that I was not being respected by her as a young man. I had older men telling me to go ahead and leave her because I didn't have to take nothing from a woman; and furthermore, I could just pay child support and not deal with her. I was ready to make that move, but first, I had to run it by my dad.

Once I finished telling my dad the situation that I was in and what I had decided to do, he looked me straight in the eyes and told me that I was going to stay right there by that young lady's side the entire nine months of her pregnancy and if I did differently, then I would have to see him in a physical way. He then stated that after those nine months if I didn't feel any different, then I could be less of a man and walk away.

I took my father's orders very seriously, and by the next school term, I was driving her to the Project Hope every morning and then meeting her halfway from the building at the end of the school day to only carry her books and walk her to the bus before I attended football practice. This was done every single day, and I gained a lot of respect from my peers and teachers for doing so. If it took me being late for practice and doing grass drills, then it was what it was because I was not going to let her go through that alone.

We decided to get baptized together, so we were able to see one another accept Christ in our lives. We were like the best of friends to each other in which we shared almost everything. It was not long before she was in the hospital preparing to have the baby, and I was more nervous than her. She was the one about to have a baby, but she was asking me was I alright and that seemed backwards to me. It made me realize that she was a strong female. Her cousin and I was there with her faithfully through all of the contractions, but the time finally came for her to be moved to the operating room for them to perform surgery. I was nervous, at first, but when I got back there in the operating room, I saw the look on her face proving that she was happy to see me. The only thing that was going through my mind when I saw her was what my dad had told me, and all I could do was thank him mentally and thank God for allowing a "real king" to raise me.

I held Denise's head while they operated on her, and the next voice I heard was our little daughter, Lyric Mattair. I felt so good to have done what a lot of grown men have often dodged doing. I was a dad, so the first person that I called was my dad to give him the good news. I talked with him over the phone while crying tears of joy. He let me know that it was all right to feel good, but the biggest challenge was ahead of me and for me to make sure that I was mentally prepared. I felt my dad on that, so I continued to play football and seek positive ways to make money. By having a good name in my community and at my school, people were willing to help me out in several ways; I just had to have the courage to ask. I did not hold back any, and I did not resort to selling drugs, but I put myself out there by asking people could I mow their lawn, work in their mechanic shops, drive them to the store, trim their hedges, and wash their cars while all along filling out job applications. Several people in the community of

Madison, white and black, helped me to be able to make some honest money. All I had to do was ask.

The entire Madison County High School faculty and staff, led by Mrs. Lou Miller, supported me in all of my endeavors around that time, and I will never forget them. I learned that people will help you if you are at least trying to help yourself. I finally landed a full-time job at this meat packaging plant called Dixie Packers. Through the help of my coaches, I was able to provide Pampers and other items for my child more consistently. I worked on the frank line where I had to lift heavy meat in freezing temperatures. It was mentally and physically challenging because of the long hours and the fact that I worked everyday around grown people and attended school daily around my peers. I knew that my childish days were over, so I cut loose all of the childish friends that I dealt with and focused on bigger and better things.

My girlfriend, Denise, was doing a great job at keeping her grades up and taking care of our daughter with the help of her mom, so I made sure that I provided them with money. When I did not have it right then, her mom, Shirley Souter, would take care of it, and I thank God for her support as well. Although it was extremely hard, I refused to miss a day from school. I refused to miss a day from work. I refused to go a day without seeing my child. I refused to let my grades drop; and I refused to let positive advice from my elders go in one ear and come out the other as much as I could help it.

I finally made it to the end of my twelfth grade year, and it was a blessing to have not given up when times got rough. While giving thanks to all of the people who helped me make it through, I walked across that stage and tightly grasped my high school diploma. I thanked my teachers for supporting me while I worked a full-time job. I thanked my coaches for not taking it easy on me. I thanked my mom, my dad, Denise's parents for not closing the doors on me, Denise for believing in me, my grandmother for keeping it real with me about the Bible, my daughter, Lyric, for keeping me motivated, and God for protecting me.

I was not able to go on the senior trip because I had to work, but that in no way affected my performance at my job because I knew that I had to take care of my daughter. After that school year was completely over, it finally dawned on me that I had made it through, and all I could do was shout for joy. I was really transitioning from a boy to a king.

The following year, Denise, my queen, walked across the very same stage, and I was there to support her. Giving the fact that dropping out of school was not even an option, both of us made it through by supporting one another and that led me to believe that obstacles are only, seemingly, insurmountable.

Chapter 2

Taking Love to a Higher Level

INTRODUCTION: *This section of my book is geared towards opening the eyes of everybody who's struggling with people telling you that you cannot do something, causing you to miss out on opportunities or lose someone who's very special to you.*

INTENTION: *My intention is to get you to realize that nine times out of ten when people tell you that you cannot do something, they are trying to keep you from growing in areas such as having more peace in your life, being wealthier, being happier, having more knowledge, etc. Do not let this world dictate how much love and energy you should place inside of anything that's important to you because the world doesn't give it to you, but it can surely assist in having it taken away.*

Believe it or not, that same girl that I met twelve years ago, when she was in the ninth grade, and I was in the tenth, are now married, and our daughter is ten-years-old. As I look back over all that we went through and the work we put out, God was the one that made it grow and last. We are now smart working parents that believe in the importance of having teamwork in all aspects of our lives such as praising God, paying bills, getting more education, investing money, giving to the less fortunate, saving money, budgeting our spending, and raising a family.

When Denise falls, I pick her up, and when I fall, she picks me up just like it was in high school. When we get in arguments with one another, we try our best to not fall asleep without clearing things up. I was always told by older guys that it is impossible to love a woman for more than a couple of years, but "oh, thank God" for my dad, not only telling me different, but living by example. I have seen a lot of men let good women walk out of their lives just to keep from changing their old ways and down the road regret doing so. I would not trade her for the world because she is truly a virtuous woman, and I refuse to let the ways of this world trick me into thinking differently.

I want to share a special part of my wedding that will remain with me for years to come. I have only heard rumors of why some men cry when they see their soon to be wife coming down the aisle, but none of those applied to me. When they opened the door for her to walk down, I looked at her, and she was so beautiful from head to toe that I could only stare. I started to think back over all the things that we had been through, all the good times we had together, all the bad times we had together, all the times we cried together, and all the times that we laughed together.

While I was thinking and staring, reality hit me and made me realize that one day I will have to lose this special person to death, and that is when the tears started to fall down my face onto the carpet of the sanctuary. I looked to the right at the junior bride's maid (my gorgeous daughter) and then back at my soon-to-be wife and made myself a promise; that since I don't know when death is going to come, I will love them both everyday as if it was the last day of their lives. So I faced the congregation, put on my shades, and took my queen hand with the intentions of exceeding the traditional marriage vows and refused to look backwards at the mistakes that were made in the past.

We have been married now for four years, and I still love her like I just met her yesterday. I now understand what Tyrone Davis was saying when he made that song, "It's So Good to be Home with You."

We travel to different places as a family, we go to church together as a family, we pray together as a family, we play games together as a family, we support all of our daughter's and nephews' events as a family, we eat dinner together as a family, and we place the love of family on a pedestal so high that the worldly things can't touch it. We don't know what the future holds for us, but we will enter it with high expectations. We have taught ourselves not to engage in unnecessary gossip and not to worry about "he say or she say" because the fact is, some people just don't want to see us happy.

I will never tell a young person that marriage is a bad thing because I am enjoying myself and if anything, I will inform them that it is vital to learn from the next person's mistakes. If the time and energy is placed in the marriage, instead of in the streets and playing little games, then it will be productive. Temptation is out there and no one is perfect; therefore, mistakes will occur, but plots are inexcusable. I thank God for my queen, I love my queen, I respect my queen, I provide for my queen, and I don't wait around until this worlds' calendar tells me to do something for her such as Valentine's Day, Christmas, Mother's Day, etc. I am not a calendar man, and I refuse to be one in the future because my wife and daughter are queen's every day of the year.

I look around and notice how some men mistreat their ladies and how some ladies mistreat their men without thinking twice about it and failing to realize that their so called "trash" can easily becomes somebody else's "treasure." My goal has always been to be the best father and the best husband on this planet through the help of God, because I got tired of seeing women abused and children abandoned.

I am almost certain that I would not love my wife, respect my wife or take care of my wife the way that I do if it weren't for me fearing God, praying, and working towards a renewed mind, and being blessed with two wonderful parents that led by example and refused to spare the rod. God is the driver of this car, and my family will continue to believe that whatever God put together, no man should be able to put asunder because we are the king and queen or our castle.

Chapter 3

A King's Presence

INTRODUCTION: This section of my book is geared towards opening the eyes of everybody who feels that a father's kingly presence or the stability in a family is not important.

INTENTION: My intention is to get you to realize that a respectful father who's absent from a child's life is robbing him or her from valuable information that can predict whether they succeed or fail on this journey. We can no longer go through life thinking that a family can consist of just a mother and child or father and child. It is time for all families to start leading by example and teaching our young about the importance of having stability and balance in the family.

So many times in this life, I have heard women say that they don't need a man and that they can do bad by themselves. Yes, I respect that coming from a woman that's being abused and mistreated, but what about the child in situations when that is not the case? Whenever a child is born into this world, we have to, as adults, base a great deal of our decisions around the welfare of that child. What might be a small impact on our lives might be a greater impact on that child's life either now or when he or she gets older.

It has to be said now or never that a child needs a father in his or her life. I often wonder if my dad was not a significant part of my life, would I be the man that I am today. Now don't get me wrong, every guy is not equipped with the tools needed to be a father; therefore, he will be more harm to the child than good.

My father stuck it out with my mom, he worked hard, he never gave up, and he respected all women. I have followed in my father's footsteps because he modeled for me, and he was a part of my daily life. I thank God for my father, and I also thank the both of them for not giving up on each other when times got rough, when funds got low, and when doors continuously closed in their faces. My father did not let the circumstances of this world cause him to slack on his responsibilities because he knew that nobody else was going to come in and take care of us. He refused to get assistance from the government if he was able to avoid it.

My father road a bicycle to work for a long period of time just to keep food on the table, he served time in the military to make something out of himself, he provided for a family of seven with only one check, until my mom was able to find a job, and we still seemed to have good holidays and birthdays. Just having him around, and seeing him go through several different situations, helped me out a great deal. He worked everyday and somehow seemed to make it to all of his kids sporting events no matter if they were home or away. I can remember being on the football field in high school and being able to spot my father out of the view of my helmet every Friday night while playing the games. My brother and I looked forward to seeing him there, and when he did come, it gave us an immeasurable amount of motivation.

The biggest thing that stands out when I think about this is the fact that he did not have to do it, but he did. I wonder if I would have witnessed my father hitting on my mom, sleeping around with several women, not coming home at night, or not supporting my sporting events, would that have influenced me? Yes, it would have; therefore, fathers need to lead by example and trash the prehistoric saying, "You do what I say, not what I do," because it is not going to happen.

Thanks father, Curtis Mattair, for being a king, because I now provide for my family. I work hard and smart. I love my wife. I respect all women, and I support my child's events. I sometimes think back to that day during high school when I wanted to leave my girlfriend when she was pregnant and settle for paying child support, but my dad was there to guide me in the right direction. I would not be feeling this way about her if I would have listened to the men of the world, but thanks to the presence of my father, because he kept me from making the biggest mistake of my life.

If you are a father reading this book and have raised your kids the best you can, I would like to say that I love you brother, and thank you for being a king because you are making this world a better place, and you are worthy of the praises. If you have not thought of your father like this, then this would be a good time to pick up the phone, write a letter, e-mail him, visit him, tell him that you love him, and thank him for not giving up on you. For the ones that have children, but did not have a father in your lives to teach you, then it is time to break that trend and give your kids what you wish you had. My father is not on a billboard, he doesn't make a million dollars a year, he is not known worldwide, he doesn't own fancy cars or a fancy home, but he is a normal, hardworking man and he is my "African American Hero." It is time that we, as parents, start thinking about the future of our children and start being their everyday heroes. Thank you God for my father's kingly presence!

Marvin "Merv" Mattair - 34

Chapter 4

A Word to My Young Kings

INTRODUCTION: *This section of my book is geared towards opening the eyes of every young king who's struggling with the pressures and temptations of this world, also the ones who have been told by others that you were not going to amount to anything.*

INTENTION: *My intention is to get you to realize that you can be whatever you desire to be on this earth as long as you apply yourself. Your actions are the only thing that can predict your future, not what people say or think about you. If there is something in life that you want, then go out there and pursue it with the confidence that you will be successful, just don't spend your life doing the same old things everyday and expect a different outcome to fall out of the sky without changing your lifestyle. Go out there and get what's yours!!!!*

In no way am I attempting to encourage young people to engage in sexual encounters through writing about my past or encourage you to try and become a man before it's time because that would not be the right thing to do. I am putting out the message that if any young person attempts to perform adult acts, then the consequences could be overwhelming, and you will have to deal with them accordingly.

My wife, Denise, and I lost a lot of our childhood days because of our decision to perform an adult act which changed our lives forever. Yes, I wanted to go on my class trips and take pictures with my class of 1997. I wanted to play college football but because of the decisions made, I wanted to focus my attention on making honest money. My wife, on the other hand, got a chance to enjoy every part of her senior year, and I was very happy for her. It was hard to accept reality at times, but I had to keep going and going. I do not regret what happened to me in my life, and I will never call my child a mistake.

All that I went through made me who I am this day. I want to encourage you, young man, to stay focused on your goals while in high school, juvenile programs, or anywhere else you may be, and don't go in being so cocky and noncompliant. I promise you, young man, that one day you will desire to make a change in your life, and if you have already made a bad name for yourself, then you will be labeled and have to wear it for a long time. My dad, pretty much, taught me that a good name is better than education any day, but both of them together are awesome. I had to seriously earn a good name through the use of respect, self-control, and discipline, but when I got it, it was well worth it.

Young man, you don't have to present yourself as a thug, a gang banger, a playboy, or a pimp just to get attention and respect; just be yourself, and if your peers can't except that, then they will get used to it. It doesn't make you look like a man whenever you cuss out a teacher or staff. It doesn't make you look like a man when you brag about the time you served in the penitentiary. It doesn't make you look like a man when you have a cigarette hanging off of your lips. It doesn't make you look like a man when you walk around with a unit on your face. It doesn't make you look like a man when you wave your gun around in the air; and it definitely doesn't make you look like a man when you abuse young women verbally and physically.

What makes you look like a young king is when you can respect yourself and everybody around you, when you can be yourself, instead of being somebody that you are not and still get respect from your peers, when you can think before you respond to situations, and when knowing better causes you to do better. I went through that phase in my life, and it got me no where very fast. I found out later in my life that a lot of the anger was displayed because of seemingly insurmountable odds that I was faced with, such as having a speech impediment and not being able to get on the same level as my peers during class. Those are not good reasons to become angry, but by me not putting forth the effort early in my life to make them better, I decided to blame everyone else except the person in the mirror. I advise you to take that very same energy that's being used for anger and use it to build up your self-esteem and confidence level, so that you can become the king that you are destined to be.

Young king, I am here to tell you that you do not have to go through this phase if you learn from my mistakes, other people's mistakes, and make wise decisions. Depending on where you live, you might not get a second chance to try it again, so take my advice. Most of the guys that got all of the attention and was so called "cool" and "hard core" in school are the ones that are now either serving time in prison, making a living selling drugs, paying child support for five or six kids, dead or either living for the love of the "streets," and the fast life. It might not be for you to have all of the attention in school, but I promise you that one day you will be recognized for your works, and you will probably be interviewing some of those very same guys in your school that got all the attention.

Young king, every decision that you make now will affect your life forever so don't go through life taking unnecessary chances. A prime example is when my younger brother, Curtis Mattair, Jr., chose to leave the town of Madison after high school to attend college at Alabama A&M, and now a few years later, he is sitting on a master's degree in Social Work and being a constant positive role model for others. If he would have decided to involve himself in adult acts or criminal acts, he might not have gotten a chance to be so successful. Also, if he would have let the opportunity of leaving his family behind to attend college slip through his fingers, he would probably be here right now working at a plant or a fast food joint only wishing that he would have taken advantage of the opportunity.

Don't be afraid of change because fear is what keeps you from being bold, and to me, boldness is one of the key ingredients of a successful brother. If fear of change is in you, please get it out now by renewing your mind or you will be idle with nothing to do but drive around your hometown and show off your new rims, sell drugs, shoot at people, hang around the clubs all night, spend time in and out of jail, and having intercourse with anybody that will allow you to. The next time you are riding in the car, take a drive by a cow field full of cows and evaluate their actions on a day-to-day basis. You are going to see the same cows walking around the same area doing the same old things while being locked in and not trying to get out and eventually will be killed.

Marvin "Merv" Mattair - 40

Young king, what differentiates a lost brother from a cow other than being human? Don't be like cows, be the young king that you are capable of being by breaking those chains that keep you in mental bondage and start doing things differently, setting goals, making plans with your life, having a say so on where you end up in the future. Soar like an eagle over every obstacle that stands in your way such as negative peers, the Florida Comprehensive Assessment Test (F.C.A.T.), drugs, violence, fear, and everything else. Think before you respond and don't respond before you think because mothers are tired of seeing their sons being buried; women are tired of losing so many brothers to the system, and little children are tired of growing up without their fathers, brothers or uncles in their lives.

It is time for a change, and guess what? The change is going to start with the man in the mirror (YOU). There is only one life that you have to live, and it is not like a pair of shoes or a piece of clothing that you can swap out, because if you lose your shoes or clothes, you can go in the closet and get another, but if you lose your life, you can't find another one in the closet. So take your life seriously.

I know that it is hard to make it in a world that promotes negative things on television, the radio, and other sources, but you have to bend those knees and ask for some help if you want to be the best that you can be. Before you go to bed at night, say a prayer; before you leave your house, pray; before you get on and off of the school bus, pray, and before you enter that school, please say a prayer. I know that this sounds like a lot of praying, but if the devil is going to stay busy, then you have to stay just as busy as he is or become a failure.

Don't wait until you get older to realize that the things of this world that look good and feel good are only temporary because it might be too late. The word of God is going to be the only thing standing, so don't waste your time trying to be friends with this world. I am only twenty-eight years of age, but I can see more clearly now and understand that all the answers to my questions are in the Bible. People can say what they want to say, but I always tell the unbeliever that it's best to believe in Him by letting it show through your actions. It's better to get to the end and find out that it was not true, than to not live right by His word, to only get to the end and find out that it was true.

Through bending my knees, reading my Bible, and learning from other people's mistakes, I have found out about the importance of silence and how much power is in it. This world has changed so greatly; therefore, you have to humble yourselves more now than ever because a lot of lives have been taken behind the power of the tongue (Proverbs 18:21). There is a time to talk and there is a time to be quiet. There is a time to react. There is a time to stand still. There is a time to go. There is a time to stay, and all of these can predict whether your future is a success, a failure, or whether you have one at all.

Every young man is not being raised in a negative environment. Every young man is not being raised by their mother alone. Every young man does not have to join a gang to feel loved. Every young man does not have to go out and sell drugs just to be able to eat. Every young man does not have to fight daily in order to survive; therefore, they should have a better chance at being successful easier and possibly faster, but if you do have to go through some of that, I want you to know that you can still make it because it is not your peers, it is not your environment, it is not your culture, and it is not your family, it is the strength and quality of your mind that predicts your future, and nobody can change that except yourself.

The reason that I know the mind is a powerful tool is through experience, so please listen to me. You don't want to see and hear everything because it will eventually start to change the way that you think, so don't hang around violent places and stop dealing so much with negative people.

I know that there are a lot of guys out there who disrespect women and treat them as if they are toys, but what does that say about them? Don't fall off into that category, young king, and if you already have, consider changing the way that you think or the people who you hang around before time runs out. Let me tell you, real men don't hit women. Real men don't call women nasty names. Real men don't have to share with another man what he and his lady do in private. Real men take care of their kids not only with money, but with their time. Real men don't have to rely on the court system to make them pay support for their kids. Real men provide their wives with not only money for the bills, but with love, honesty, trust, passion, and quality time. Real men don't sit around on their bottoms and watch things happen; they get off of their butts and make things happen. Lastly, a real man will stand up for what is right.

Respect the young queens at all times and stop listening to guys who tell you that it is okay and that is normal to mistreat them. I want you to realize that one day you are probably going to have a daughter, and you are not going to want her to be mistreated by a young man. Ask yourself this question, what if my daughter, sister, or mother comes home and states that a young man has just forcibly rubbed on their body and cursed them out, how would you feel? I would not feel good about that; therefore, it needs to be known that everybody has someone that loves them, so they should never be mistreated intentionally by you, because what goes around comes around. Don't waist your time running behind every girl and woman who you see in a pair of tight jeans because everything that looks good is not, believe me.

Young man, if you play around enough, then you will eventually run up on a baby and from that point on you will have to change your lifestyle. Whatever your future plans were, they will be altered due to the fact that you will have greater responsibilities on hand. Don't drop out of school. Instead, talk to someone that has a sense of what you are going through and continue to try your best. Your dreams can still come true, but it will indeed take greater effort with a kid on your side. It will seem easier to just walk away, but it will only hurt you in the future, financially and mentally.

See, you might not have a king in your life that's going to keep you from making the biggest mistake in your life, so I am here to tell you not to hurt that young lady and not to be absent from that kid's life. Life is similar to a game of checkers. If you make an impulsive and poorly thought out move, you will have to wait around until the door opens up again for you to redeem yourself; but, in the mean time, you are losing a lot of your pieces from that bad decision, causing it to be harder and more difficult to reach your goal whether it's a crown on the checkerboard table or a crown of recognition on your head for being a successful young king in life. Now if you were to take out the time to think three moves ahead before responding, you would have a greater chance of reaching your goals. I learned from experience that responding before thinking only leads to 100% failure.

I did not start North Florida Community College of Madison, Florida, until I was twenty-five-years-old because of my high school experiences, but I was ready mentally and physically when I finally started. See, my plans were to get straight out of high school and attend college, but I had too many responsibilities so I started a few years after, and I couldn't have started at a better time. I applied myself, and I received several awards for academics and leadership, such as the Dean's List, President of the African American Student Union Leadership Award in 2004 and 2005 and several more, but it shocked me when I saw my face being advertised in the college magazines over and over.

I got a chance to speak about one of our club events on the WCTV morning news station which was something new to me and very challenging. Out of all of those awards and opportunities, the most rewarding one came when I took a trip to a different county to take care of some bills, and I noticed my face on a big billboard beside the highway, advertising for NFCC. That was big for me, and it became even bigger when I found out that there was a billboard placed in several surrounding counties. That was like my first time ever seeing a college billboard that placed an African American male wearing locked hair on it around this area, but it dawned on me that I had established a good name for myself over the years, and the wonderful people at that college recognized it.

It was only a picture to some people, but to me, it was a young man that was making his dreams come true. Currently, I work at a juvenile camp where I counsel young men, so I keep that picture of me posted on the wall of my office for encouragement and for the young men to see that anything is possible as long as they apply themselves. I tell them that they might not get what they want when they want it, but be patient and it will come. I was able to do it, and I'm currently doing it so that should let you know that if I can do it, then so can you but probably better.

Young man, you might not be a big time superstar making millions of dollars, but if you establish a good name for yourself it will help out a great deal. I found out that it don't take a person on television to give good advice, anyone can give it as long as it comes from the heart and through experience. For example, there was an older guy in my hometown, named Mr. Ruben, who used to sell hot dogs from his hot dog stand that was adjacent to the downtown post office and the court house buildings. I did not know the guy's name at first, but he was known around town as the Hot Dog Man, so that is what I called him whenever I bought from him. It got to the point, that every time I spent money at the post office, I would support his business as well by purchasing a slaw dog. I would just stop by his stand sometimes, my daughter and I, just to talk with him because he was my elder, and he would always tell me about the old days and how far we have come.

When Mr. Ruben took sick, my daughter and I went by his home to visit him one day to make sure that he was okay. Even though he was going through something, he took out his time and told me, "Merv, whatever you go through in this life, good or bad, or whatever you receive such as houses, cars, businesses, pay raises, or whatever you have, never forget to tell God thank you." Shortly after that, Mr. Ruben passed on, but those words will always be in my mind and in my heart.

The Hot Dog Man gave me a different outlook on life; therefore, he is considered one of my African American Heroes. Those words of wisdom were not found in the big post office or in the court house so don't take for granted that someone who lives under a bridge or under cardboard can become your hot dog man and change your perspective on life forever. God will use anybody to keep you from falling flat on your face. All you have to do is be receptive (the accepting of what's giving to you). I don't have a big time degree up under my belt, and I am not rushing it. I am only a brother who loves you and who doesn't want you to give up on your dreams, no matter what the circumstances are. No matter what your dreams are, always remember that you, almost all the time, have to give up something to get something.

Marvin "Merv" Mattair - 50

I have always loved to listen to music, but when my life took a different route, I thought that I would not be able to find a type of music that I could relate to. I did not feel the older gospel songs, and I got tired of hearing about negative things through some of the rap songs because it was affecting my thinking. I can now say, thank you, God, for artists such as Kirk Franklin, Dietrich Haddon, J. Moss, George Huff, Fred Hammond, The Gospel Tru Tones, and Latresha Wilson of Madison, Florida, Martha Munizzi, Lexi, Rizen, Tonex, Yolanda Adams, Ty Trebbett, Kanye West, Alicia Keys, Anthony Hamilton, and many more because their music encourages me daily as a young father and husband trying to live right.

Find out what motivates you as a young king, in a positive way, and spend more time doing it, and I promise you that you will soon forget about the negative. I am a strong believer of whatever the majority of your time is spent doing defines who you are as a person. So young man, drop the guns, drop the drugs, drop all of the violence, drop the negativity, and pick up books, and all other positive items that will help towards the process of renewing your mind because if you don't make it, you can't blame no one but yourself. I love you, and I want you to strive to be a king instead of another statistic!

to start with our young women. I have observed a great deal of obstacles over the course of my life that stands in the way of our young ladies transforming into mature women, and I will be the first one to say that enough is enough. ,

Young queen, whenever you lower your standards to please a young man, you have just set yourself up for failure. If you keep your standards high, and he is not willing to get on your level, he is not worthy of being with you. But if he is willing to get on your level, he will become a better man through you not making it so easy for him. You don't have to be intimate with a young man for him to respect you and like you because he will respect you more if you carry yourself in a mature manner by letting him know that you don't get down like that; now he might not like it, but again, he will respect you. You don't have to be like the other girls, just be yourself and that will pay off in the long run.

I don't want you, young lady, to think just because my wife and my situation worked out for the best that yours will be the same. So don't get that impression. It might turn out better or it might turn out worse. You need to make wise decisions. When you are in school you are there to learn, not to impress the older boys through wearing extra tight or revealing clothing, causing them to want you for what is on the outside instead of for what is in your heart. I have seen a large number of young ladies lose it mentally to the streets and forget about school and the respect that they should have for their parents by cursing at them, not coming home at night, embarrassing them in front of their friends, and taking their peers advice over theirs.

You don't even realize that if your parents decide to stop providing for you, that will lead you to seeking assistance from your so called "home girls" or family members, and I promise you that none of them will love you like your parents do, depending on the circumstances. Don't be fooled by the videos and the songs that encourage you to make stupid decisions or use your temples for fun and games just to make a quick buck because it will indeed come back to haunt you. I am tired of seeing our gorgeous queens misuse their temples while being young, so that when they decide to change their lives, as they get older, they are bound down with children from different men or their business is spread all across town and on the Internet making it harder to be trusted or respected by a potential good man.

During the high school days, my wife always had respect for her body through dressing properly and not trying to keep up with the latest fads. If she would have dressed provocatively, then I would have probably wanted her for what she could perhaps do, not for who she was. The last thing you want is to become pregnant by a person that you was just having a good time with or just trying to please or impress, so protect your temple. You don't want to be carrying a baby from someone that you don't intend on being with for the rest of your life, so don't make that mistake. Don't let down your guard and start to think that it is easy to take care of a child just because you see other girls doing it because I can tell you, for a fact, that the young man is not going to be the one to wake up in the middle of the night to change diapers and fix bottles, you are, so I encourage you not to go that route until you are out of high school and established in your life.

If for some reason it happens to you while being in school, don't drop out of school, and don't let yourself go down physically or mentally because you can still make it. Keep your head up, and don't be afraid to ask for help, talk to someone who has gone through it before. Just don't put the full responsibility off on someone else because that will easily cause you to become irresponsible.

While you are young, you have full control of your future with the guidance of God, so don't let the pressures, and the temptations of this world cause you to go astray. I hear a lot of women on the radio and television talking about wanting to have a man that is a certain height, a certain weight, makes a certain amount of money, and that should not be the case. Don't fall into that trap because the right man for you might not have everything that you're looking for but a lot of what you need.

I can inform you that if you notice a young man not respecting his mom and other females, don't think that he is going to respect you after the honeymoon period is over. If he doesn't have fear of a higher power (God) then what you don't see is not going to bother his conscience. Men are visual creatures; therefore, you are always being watched by someone perverted and up to no good whether you know it or not. So be careful of what you wear, who you talk with, and where you go because times have changed, and you need to think before you respond.

Don't let the large amounts of money fool you. Don't let the fancy cars fool you. Don't let the free shopping sprees fool you. And don't let anyone fool you into thinking that you should be their lover on the side because if you are indeed a queen, then you should always be number one. You are somebody that does not have to settle for less in any situation as long as you present yourself as a queen at all times.

I encourage you, young lady, while you are young, to get an interest in something such as college, reading, sports, traveling, or you will become an adult still chasing behind men and wondering why you can't let go. As long as you have a family that care about your well being, please take advantage of that and learn all that you can before you step out there and attack this world because honestly, this world doesn't care about you failing, succeeding, being happy, or being sad. You deserve to be happy and very successful, so set goals for yourself, follow your dreams, don't let the ways of this world bring you down, reach for the stars, take a chance at being abnormal and never forget to Always-Say-A-Prayer (A.S.A.P).

Chapter 6

The Key Ingredients to a Royal Life

INTRODUCTION: *This section of my book is geared towards opening the eyes of every person who has inherited the wrong ingredients of royal living. Nobody has to live a life of hate, negativity, or violence if they chose not to, so don't be fooled by foolish people. Think about it, if a professional baker gives you the ingredients to bake a good cake, but you place the wrong ingredients inside of it, will it turn out like it should? No, it will not, so what make people think that they can pour anything into their only life and have it turn out like the Potter planned it to? Too much milk will mess up a good cake just like being exposed to too much negativity will mess up a good life.*

INTENTION: *After reading this, you will know the key ingredients to royal living; therefore, worldly circumstances should not be able to dictate your future thoughts or actions.*

If you were to break down the word LIFE, you would see that the letter (L) stands for <u>Love</u>. You can earn all of the college degrees that you want. You can make all of the money that's out there to be made. You can have the fanciest cars and homes, but if you don't have love in your heart for yourself and your fellow man, then you really don't have anything. In order to love someone else, you need to love yourself first, and be mindful to treat others how you want to be treated.

The letter (I) stands for <u>Investing</u> your time and money into places that are going to benefit you. Investing your time in the gym, with your family, in your Bible, in church, by yourself, and doing things that you like, will contribute to royal living. Investing your money into mutual funds, annuities, land, or any other place that will allow your money to increase instead of decreasing will create less stress in a marriage and also make it so that when you are retired, you don't have to suffer financially.

The letter (F) stands for <u>Fellowshipping</u> with people who think almost identical to the way that you think, in a positive way. I don't care if it's family or friends, if they can contribute to your mental growth, take advantage of it, but whoever cannot, needs to be cut loose. Why would someone who loves their spouse and who takes pride in the family life hang out consistently with someone who thinks the total opposite? Unless you are trying to do God's work with them, you are setting yourself up for failure. Fellowshipping with people who think like you will give you a sense of comfort, motivation, encouragement, and mental growth unlike someone who thinks the total opposite.

The letter (E) stands for <u>Enjoyment</u>, but as you see, it is the last letter of the word LIFE; therefore, it has to be earned. If you love yourself and your fellowman, you will invest your time and your money in places that will benefit you and not hurt you. Then, you will fellowship with people who can help to keep you thinking that way or probably better, so you won't have any reason not to enjoy your life. Now once you get to the point of enjoying your life, don't forget about God and definitely don't forget where you came from because one phone call, one layoff, or one accident can change your life forever.

You have to start the process of renewing your mind while you are young because the older you get, the harder it will be to accept the fact that your way of thinking is wrong. If you let this world system guide your thinking, I promise you that you will end up in the future blaming everyone else for your downfalls instead of realizing that you were ultimately responsible.

Just stop for a minute or two and look around to see how the ways of this world have taken people's minds off of some important areas in life such as health and responsibility. I say health because there are a lot of men and women that have nice looking and very expensive cars that they put the best gas in, the best oil, the best parts on, and refuse to put anything harmful in it or on it, but yet, they put drugs and other harmful substances in their body as if the car is more important than their temples.

We have to start taking care of our bodies a little better by performing regular tune-ups on them, just like we do the expensive cars and other materialistic items. We have to eat right. We have to exercise regularly. We have to read daily. And we have to try our best to stay in good spirits, instead of having so much hate in our hearts. It is time that we start putting our money toward foods that are good for us rather than good to us. If we don't take care of our bodies, who will? I will be the first to say that exercising is not something easy to do consistently; therefore, I recommend Cardio4Christ, a group of powerful and positive people from Huntsville, Alabama, who show you how to exercise and give God praise while doing so. They may be reached at: cardio4christ@gmail.com .

I say responsibility because we allow fads to get in the way of the bigger picture of our actual living. There is so much money being spent on shoes, clothes, fancy rims, and jewelry which may only be in style for a short period of time, yet instead, hundreds and hundreds and sometimes thousands of dollars are being spent on these items by individuals. The message has got to be put out there that when a young person start making money, they should start investing at least some of it in their future.

When I started working at Dixie Packers during my high school years, the price of land was $20,000 cheaper than what it is now, but I failed to pursue this. I did not know that one day I would want to get a house built. If I would have just listened to my elders more, instead of living for the moment, I would have saved and made a lot more money than what I did, but I settled for the rims, the jewelry, and the biggest speakers in my trunk. 'The Power of People' had me so far gone because none of that stuff was for me, it was for the people to see, hear, and comment on. Everyone does things for different reasons, just be honest with yourself, so that you can move forward with the renewing of your mind.

Some people are born into money and into businesses but others have to work hard and work smart for what they get. My young people, don't be fooled by what you see on television, and don't worry about what the next man got because everybody has their season, and yours is right around the corner. Just keep the faith. If you want to live a royal life, then I encourage you to take advantage of the ingredients mentioned while on the journey of renewing your mind.

Chapter 7

Becoming a King

INTRODUCTION: *This section of my book is geared towards opening the eyes of every young married man or soon-to-be married man who struggles with identifying who you are and what is expected of you as a king. You have to take a pause in your life to acknowledge the fact that you are not doing the very best that you can. I feel that nobody should be able to wear the title "Man" or "King" on this earth until they have proven themselves to be one. Do you think that just because people can give good CPR (cardiopulmonary resuscitation) that they will be allowed to call themselves a doctor? I don't think so; therefore, I feel that the title "man" should not be placed on someone just because they can produce an offspring. If the title was earned, then there would be a lot of guys taken out of the lineup.*

INTENTION: After reading this, you will know the basics of how to be a man who is the king of your family. You will love your wife for the queen that she is, and you will also love your kids and be a role model for them instead of passing the responsibility elsewhere.

We, as adults, sometime get this word man confused, and by us misrepresenting it, our young men will continue to carry it on. It is time that we set the record straight on what a man is. We have so long heard men say that God wants a man to provide for his family and work hard. That is true, but let me dissect the word provide so that it will be cleared up. When we, men, provide for our wives and families, we are providing them with love, trust, honesty, friendship, and respect. When we see our wives cleaning the house, it is not going to hurt for us to get our hands dirty too, knowing that stress causes a high number of deaths in women.

When she is in the kitchen cooking us a meal, it will not hurt us to put the bread in the oven for her or stir the beans. When she has a problem and need someone to talk to, it is not going to hurt us to listen to her even if it takes longer than usual. When our kids need that physical support for any reason, we have to be ready, willing, and able to come to their rescue with our time, and not just money through the mail. This is the age of accountability. I am tired of guys wearing the title of a man, but not holding down the responsibilities that come along with it. No, it is not written down anywhere that a man has to hold his woman's hand in public or open the door for her when she is getting in and out of the car, but what is wrong with doing that? That simple gesture will probably make your woman's day, and it doesn't cost you anything.

I am tired of seeing so many hardworking, respectful, and God fearing women walking around with frowns on their faces because we don't want to take out the time to supply them with their needs and wants. Guys, if we go all out for our queens by doing things differently, think about the effect that we will have on our marriages and the younger gentlemen that watch us daily. If the queen of your life smell's good, then tell her. If she look's nice in that outfit, tell her. If it tastes like she stuck her foot in that Sunday meal, tell her. If you are proud of her for taking care of the kids, tell her. Don't waste any time discussing the negative things, yet instead, say things that will motivate her because her daily duties exceed yours.

Men, it is time that we not preach or talk about it, but show our young kings how to love a queen, how to work and make honest money, how to take care of their kids, how to be respectful, and responsible through our actions. I know that it is hard for us, men, at times to deal with all of this temptation that this world has to offer, but we have to do a better job at fellowshipping with the right people and stop making excuses. If we go to the club and get drunk, yes, expect something foul to happen. If we are constantly talking on the cell phone with another woman, yes, expect something foul to eventually happen. If we stay out all times of the night with our partners, yes, expect something foul to eventually happen. If we spend more time with our homeboys than we do with our wives, yes, expect something foul to happen. And if we spend our lives thinking that it is just easier to pay child support instead of spending time with our children, indeed, something foul will eventually happen.

We have to wash our hands with foolishness and start looking at the bigger picture. We can no longer let the gorgeous women on television change the way that we feel about our wives because, I promise you, if we place makeup on our queens and reveal them to the world, they will quickly become popular as well. We can no longer disrespect women and become angry when another man disrespects our daughters. And we should not have to sound a trumpet when we take our wives shopping, or when we cook them a fancy meal, or when we treat them like a queen because the world will know that our wives are taken care of through the way that they smile, the way that they look, the way that they act, and the amount of times that they use our names in their daily conversations with friends and family. Real men, if you feel me, stand up and make yourself known because this world, our children, and our queens need us to be kings.

Chapter 8

Living Dr. King's Dream

INTRODUCTION: This section of my book is geared towards opening the eyes of every African American who can't seem to understand the reason that our culture is not moving forward as a whole.

INTENTION: After reading this chapter, you will know why our children struggle so much with understanding what's real and what's fake. You will learn the reason our culture is not moving forward as a whole, and you will realize just why it's time to stand up now and speak out on what's right, and stop worrying about the adversary. The future of our culture is in our hands.

The time has come that we, as African Americans, evaluate ourselves and ask the question, what am I doing to contribute to the betterment of our culture? We can no longer sit back and take a free ride off of Dr. King's accomplishments because if we do, fifteen years from now, our kids will be discussing the very same, "I Have a Dream Speech," that has not become a full reality. We have to look in the mirror and ask ourselves, what am I doing for my culture? Or do I even care where we are when our kids are older?

Children these days have been blamed for a great deal of the chaos in this world when they shouldn't be. I am here to tell you that adults are the reason that our culture is lacking the respect, self-control, and discipline that should be prominent in all aspects of our lives. We can have all sorts of programs to help better the thoughts and actions of our young kings and queens, but as long as our African American adults don't lead by example, then we are not going to move forward. I have worked with young juvenile men for the past eight years at one of the top facilities in the state of Florida, and it is sad to say that after some of the young men leave the program with great changes made in their lives, their parents have not made any in theirs and the child ends up back in the same environment with high chances of relapsing. How can you blame the kid when no one is providing them with structure, stability, or discipline? You can't; therefore, we have a great deal of Achan's in our culture that keeps us from reaching higher heights on this earth as a whole and until they change their ways, things are going to only get worse.

In the Bible when the Israelites were not able to go forward with their progress due to losing a battle, they stopped to evaluate themselves. They wondered why they were not able to be successful like they knew they should be, and it came to them that one person in their tribe, by the name of Achan, had not done right. He had gone against the planned mission of the tribe that was set by God. Once they got rid of him, they were able to move forward again, so what does that tell us? We have a great deal of Achan's in our culture who are not contributing to the planned mission of Dr. King and other leaders, and until they start doing the right things, our culture is going to stand in one spot as a whole.

There are a few areas that I have observed over the past couple of years that's causing us to struggle more than we have to, and it is time that it's made known. These areas are as followed:

family, churches, church folk, media, and professionals such as actors, rappers, radio hosts, athletes, and comedians.

Family. The family is where kids should be taught the basics such as social skills, respect, self-control, and discipline for surviving on this earth. There are several things in the family system that have changed for the worse, and it is causing a problem for everybody. The first problem is that we don't show enough love to one another; therefore, our youth search for it through gangs and the streets. Instead, we wait until someone is deceased before we have something good to say about them. If we just take out the time to call our family and tell them that we love them while they are living, that will mean more to them to hear it now, instead of saying it when they are deceased.

We, as family, have to teach our kids about the power of love and that nothing else can compare to it. I think that the dinner table is not being used as much as it used to for the purpose that it was built for anymore. It's so bad now that commercials had to be aired in an attempt to get families to utilize their own dinner tables. A lot of dinner tables see more playing cards than they do plates of food. The dinner table is where the family can discuss anything and where kids learn valuable skills. When parents refuse to teach their kids the basics at home such as respect, self-control, discipline, honesty, love, and boundaries, it makes it hard for anybody who crosses that kid's path, especially school teachers. I don't find it funny when some parents laugh whenever their kid curse, when they allow their kid to touch on other people's children, and then support them, and when they allow their kids to hang around whomever without meeting them first.

Although parents were getting into a lot of trouble for abusing their children all over the world, my mom and dad did not let that stop them from whipping our back sides. They knew that they were doing what was beneficial to all of us. They did not abuse us verbally or physically, but they were consistent with the consequences without fear of this world's system. I can admit that I strayed away from what I was taught, but I can also confess that it did not take me long to come back.

Just because the state took prayer out of the schools doesn't mean that we, as parents, can't teach our kids how to pray on their own. Today, families are letting the ways of this world dictate what they do and don't do, and it is only tearing down the family structure. The family is not as big on spending time or supporting one another like they should. The family man is not being in control of his house, but yet, he tries to hold down another man's house, causing his son to follow in his footsteps. The family mom stresses herself out with life situations and begin to lose all of her self-esteem, causing her daughter to follow in her footsteps.

Mom and dad have got to let go of the negative ways of this world by loving each other unconditionally, spending time with one another, buying each other gifts other than on holidays and birthdays, playing and joking to keep the laughter present, standing strong together through all obstacles, and supporting each other's dreams to show all onlookers, and your kids that marriage can be a very good thing. The family has got to put down that worldly calendar and start giving and showing love other than on Christmas, spending family time together other than on Thanksgiving, and showing appreciation other than on Valentine 's Day. We have been making excuses as to why we can't do certain things for years, and now it has come to the point of accountability. If we, as African Americans, refuse to put the value of family on a pedestal, then we will not be able to contribute to the betterment of the African American culture; therefore, there will continue to be Achan's causing the trend to not be broken.

Churches and church folk. The church has been the place for people to enjoy great music, hear the truth about the heavenly Father, change their lives, and sow seeds. Some churches and some church folks have strayed away from the biblical mission and it is greatly affecting the culture. Whatever our young people see us doing, they are going to think that it is the correct way of doing things, and then they will carry it on as a tradition. We are all judgmental people, but church folks have run a lot of lost souls out of the house of God for different reasons, failing to realize that they were not always the way that they are.

Some church folks come in and pray a good prayer, sing a good song, and leave the service to only be of the world through gossiping, unnecessary cursing, cheating, and lying. Some of them will pay their tithes and offerings in the presence of others, but when it comes to helping someone, when there are not that many people around, they refuse to do so. The Bible is straightforward, but it is being played with, and people don't realize the harm that they are doing when they know better by reading God's word, but refuse to do better. A great deal of church folks gossip about each other and they feel that God is okay with that, and they have hate in their heart and feel that God is okay with that also, but He is not. Some church folk have used the word predestination as a crutch and an excuse to keep from making a change in their lives. I witnessed all of this from the time that I was able to understand things up to this point in my life.

Some churches have gone from what they were, to a business that is in competition with other churches. Instead of working together, a lot of them separate themselves to keep from having to share the funds or the recognition. A great deal of people are not being themselves or not using their talents. Instead, they try to do whatever it takes to fit in or be accepted by man. Some people only read what their pastor preach about in service that day and fail to go home and further their education; therefore, their knowledge is limited to what's discussed in church.

I am not intentionally criticizing the church, but I know that if I noticed all of these things growing up and they are still going on, the young people today will also notice it. If this continues to go on, then the younger people will carry this on as a tradition, and it will not be for the betterment of our African American Culture; therefore, there will continue to be Achan's causing us to be in a paused state.

The media, professionals such as rappers, radio hosts, athletes, and comedians. The television, the radio, and the Internet are places that we, as humans, can turn to for entertainment and information. We have actually benefited from these sources over the years, but we have also suffered mentally behind some of their contents. We, as adults, have always blamed the young men and the young women for their actions, but we fail to realize that children are not responsible for allowing sex to be aired on the television, profanity, and sexual conversations to be aired over the radio stations.

I was very upset when a local radio station made a joke about Mr. Ray Charles after his death and kept it going as if it was okay. I can recall at the end of the movie, Barber Shop, when there were jokes made about Mrs. Rosa Parks. I was surprised to know that our own kind could find that funny. How can our young kings and queens even start to appreciate the efforts that our African American ancestors contributed to the betterment of their future if the adults are making fun of them? We have to act our age and realize that everything cannot be made out of a joking matter. I can think back on several fights and immature things professional athletes have done to the point that it makes you appreciate the Barry Sanders and Michael Jordan's of the leagues.

Someone can commit a murder or break a law and become famous by adults making it out of a movie just to make a profit. I can't see any other reason that they would want to teach viewers how to commit a crime. I have heard rappers in their music speak about selling drugs, killing another person, robbing the poor, dropping out of school, disrespecting our soul brothers, disrespecting our soul sisters, and avoiding living a family life. I feel that there is nothing wrong with a person feeling a certain way because of how they were raised, but when they are allowed to spread it across the world, that is when it becomes a problem.

There is no way that responsible parents can fully keep that foolishness out of their homes and from around their kids; therefore, they are exposed to it. Whatever happened to only playing adult songs and movies late at night when the children are in bed? The bad thing is that there are songs that are geared towards young people fighting in the club. There are songs geared towards young people getting their guns and shooting another. There are songs geared towards young people doing and selling drugs for a quick come up. And there are songs geared towards young people viewing sex as a hobby. How can our culture move forward if the people who our kids look up to don't send out a positive message? What are our kids supposed to think when the people who send out the negative messages are seen on television receiving awards and being praised?

We can be our own worst enemy at times, but the love of money keeps us from recognizing it. All of these sources of entertainment and information are governed by adults, and not children; therefore, whenever the adults start doing things differently, then this world will be a better place to stay. Greed has taken over and people are trying to get money any way possible, even if it takes them poisoning a child's mind. I feel that unnecessary negativity through the media is a legalized drug that does more harm to the mind of our people, even more so than illegal substances. Please start making changes today, starting with the man in the mirror. Thanks.

Chapter 9

My Renewed & Improved Mind

I had to pray for and pursue a renewed mind because I wanted to be the person that God desired me to be. I could no longer let the power of the streets and temptations of this world direct my path and dictate my actions, but while I was out there, I don't regret some of the things that I did or some of the people who I met because those were the weights that got me as strong as I am today. In order for me to be complete on my royal journey, there were a few desires of my heart that had to be fulfilled. I desired to love my wife like she has never been loved before. I desired to love, protect, and teach my child like parents are supposed to do. I desired to respect all of my brothers and sisters, white, black, and others just like I wanted to be respected. I desired to have my biological name represent who I am and what I have done instead of some college degree. I desired to respect every woman for who she is and not for what she could do. I desired to stand up for what is right no matter how others took it.

I desired to be able to give to the less fortunate every opportunity that I got without expecting anything in return. I desired to grow older and be able to tell friends, co-workers, family members, especially my mother and father, that I love them while looking them straight in the eyes. I desired to give people their flowers while they are living instead of when they are deceased. I desired to utilize the power of silence and cease unnecessary talking and rambling. I desired to not be embarrassed to pray at any given time. I desired to take my health very seriously and stay in great shape so that I can run around with the young during activities. I desired to learn from my elders by keeping my mouth shut and listening while they are talking. I desired to be able to tell my wife daily that she looks gorgeous, and that I love her. I desired to not be afraid to tell a young person to do right when they are doing wrong.

I desired to be able to spend the majority of my time off the job with my family instead of with peers. I desired to not waste money on foolish items, but invest it in places that are going to benefit my family in the future since I don't know what tomorrow holds. I desired to go through life not just learning from my own mistakes all the time, but when possible, learn from the next man's mistakes.

I desired to be myself and not let what man think about me change that. I desired to have a bigger heart in the area of giving rather than receiving. I desired to overlook the holidays and treat everyday as if it was Christmas, Thanksgiving, Valentine's Day, Mother's Day, and Father's Day. I desired to give thanks to our African American leaders in my hometown, such as teachers, preachers, bus drivers, and parents that are paving the way but never getting recognized for doing so. I desired to teach my child about racism and the fact that white people got beaten and killed also in attempt to bring slavery to an end, so it is important to love everyone. I desired to appreciate the struggles in my life instead of complaining about them. I desired to seek education for what I will learn and not for what I will earn on a job. I desired to read my Bible from the beginning, so that I could understand the full journey, and I desired to make reading my number one hobby instead of sports.

Praying for what I wanted and putting forth the effort, allowed me to receive a renewed mind, and I love every minute of it. If I would have let this world continue to direct my path, I would have probably ended up in a casket at a young age or a lover of the streets, thinking that royalty was more physical than mental. Please pray that I continue to let the reading and understanding of the Bible show through my daily actions that I may love my family, and continue to have love in my heart and spread this message to my young kings and queens all across this world.

Chapter 10

My Prayer

Father God, thank you for life. Thank you for family. Thank you for strength, courage, and wisdom. Thank you for good health. Thank you for my wife. Thank you for my child. Thank you for the food that you have allowed to be placed on my table, the clothes on my back, the air that I breath, the shoes on my feet, the roof over my head, and for a renewed mind.

Father God, when this world gets me down so low that I want to give up, continue to make me realize that I am only getting stronger, and that I have a purpose. If I do indeed depart from You for any reason, please pull me back in because I can't live without knowing that You are a part of my daily decisions.

Father God, bless us and make it known to every man that if they are only talking about making a difference in this world, but not putting forth the effort, that they need to sit down, shut up, and

Marvin "Merv" Mattair - 88

quit wasting the precious gift of air that You provide us with. Father, continue to use me in any way You see fit, and keep me from attempting to fit in with worldly people because You have been too good to me, and You have brought me too far for me to turn around. When I am faced with temptation in my life, continue to make me realize that what this world has to offer cannot compare to what You have already given me and plan on giving me in the future. Prepare my heart Father to deal with any criticism that will come behind the writing of this book.

Father God, please place Your shield around me, and keep me in the battle. Make me realize, Father, that this renewed mind that I have is not a destination, but a never ending journey; therefore, I should be on a different level tomorrow and constantly growing the rest of the days to follow.

I Love You, Father.

AMEN.

Acknowledgements

I would, first of all, like to thank God for blessing me with life health and strength. For renewing my mind and for showing me that I don't have to be someone else just to fit in with the crowd. It is an honor to give thanks to my mom and dad, Shirley & Curtis Mattair, for raising me the right way and not giving up on one another even when times got rough. Mom, whether you knew it or not, you motivated me to get back in college when I saw you walk across that college stage a few years ago as a mom with five grown children. You two keep God first and stay alive because it is a blessing to see your faces. Grandparents: R.I.P Rommie Jonas, Flora Kelly, and Catherine Murphy. My godsons: Marcus Jr. and Zarion. My brothers and sisters: Curtis Mattair, Jr., Kelvin Mattair, Elshauntey Mattair, Rosaline Mattair, and Shantel Wise. Brother and sister-in-laws: R.I.P Jody Joseph, Choya Wise, Tosheba Joseph, Lyndell Mattair, Elayne Weatherspoon, and Jimmy Weatherspoon. Mother and father-in-laws: Shirley Souter (I truly thank God for you a hundred times over again), Carlton Souter (A.K.A Big Man, I love you brother, and I thank you for everything that you have done for me, my wife, and my daughter) and Clenon Joseph, Sr. (Thanks for accepting me). I would like to spread a word of love to all of my nieces and nephews and to all of my family members in Gainesville, Florida, Lake Butler, Florida, Orlando, Florida, Tallahassee Florida, Live Oak, Florida, Madison, Florida, and Alabama.

I would like to thank my cousin Pedro from Gainesville, Florida. For giving me the nickname Merv over twenty years ago because I would have never pulled that out of Marvin, so for everybody that was curious about that name, there is your answer, I love you big cousin.

I give thanks to all of the teachers that have worked with me over the years in Madison, Florida, especially my former instructor Andrea Oliver of North Florida Community College because she was not only an instructor, she was a mentor and a counselor to me. I thank all of my 1996 high school football teammates (Cowboys) for eventually accepting the fact that I had to separate myself mentally in order to make something out of myself. To all of my friends and co-workers, I thank you for showing me love when I needed it. To Mrs. Zandra Jones for approving these words, and encouraging me to take them further. And for all the young men that I have worked with, thanks for allowing me to bless you with my knowledge and wisdom. Guys, don't give up on your dreams and always remember that there is a great deal of power in silence.

I thank all of the churches and schools that allowed me to come and bless them with my words, and all of the youth that received a blessing.

Last but not least, I want to thank my wife, Denise Mattair, and my daughter, Lyric Mattair, for not giving up on me while I constantly try to better my future, for respecting me as a king, for supporting my events, and for keeping me focused. You two are so important to me, and I want you to know that I love the both of you so very much, and no matter what happens in the future, never drop your guards to the ways of this world. Thank you for reading this book.

I love you all.

Marvin "Merv" Mattair
Author

I want to commend Marvin "Merv" Mattair for such an outstanding testimony. It is through testimonies like this, that men who are men are left no other opportunity but to assume responsibility. I am so awestruck by the way Marvin has laid this material out, especially for our young men. It is amazing how many young men we are losing because they do not want to assume responsibility for the matters they created. In one of my sermons, I spoke on the fact that men run away from families because they see family as work. When young men become married or engaged in a relationship, all they consider is what good can come from it. Hardly ever do they consider what they will have to put into it. They negate the fact that bills have to be paid, children have to be raised, and incidentals happen. All of this requires them to work. Since work is a negative word to them, they run to anything (more times than none a woman) that doesn't require them to put forth any effort. We must, as Marvin is attempting to, reach out to our young men of today's world and let them know that there is yet hope.

I admire Marvin for being bold to share with the world the situations he encountered in life that made him the wonderful man he is today. Everyone encounters situations. As a basketball coach, I often tell my athletes that it's not the mistake that kills you, it's what you do after the mistake. Marvin is a prime example of this and many more men can be also. Marvin has exampled for our young men that mistakes will come and as long as you live, you will make them. What you do after that mistake is the determining factor in your success or failure.

Just as in the church we are to learn from the life of the children of Israel. See their follies, shortcomings, stepping stones, and bridges and live better. I want to highly commend Marvin "Merv" Mattair for such an outstanding job.

Marcus Hawkins, Pastor
Shiloh Missionary Baptist Church
Madison, Florida

Mr. Mattair demonstrates maturity beyond his years in the advice and counsel he offers young people on how to grow into adulthood and take responsibility for their actions. He cites the pitfalls of destructive activities that limit real growth and opportunity and bind young people to a life of poverty and hopelessness. But he also offers hope and encourages young people to steer their lives away from temptation and toward promise and enlightenment.

He uses his own life as an example to learn from, and he credits his parents, both his mother and his father, for the extremely positive impact they had in his development and maturity. The book is timely and full of good advice for young people. I strongly recommend it to any young person who is looking for a roadmap to a better life.

Morris G. Steen, Jr., President
North Florida Community College
Madison, Florida

It gives me great pleasure to highly recommend this wonderful and inspiring book, *Words to My Kings & Queens: Achieving a Renewed & Improved Mind,* by Marvin Mattair. This book is packed with personal testimonies and advice suitable for the reader of every age, race, and gender with a message for everyone who has a compassionate heart.

I have encountered hundreds of students in the course of my teaching career, but one that I continue to hold in highest esteem is Marvin Mattair. He was a student in my second grade class nearly twenty two years ago, and he continues to be a shining star. Then, as now, Marvin has always shown love, interest, and concern for others in that he lives the true meaning of the Golden Rule... *"Do unto others as you would have them do unto you."* His Christian values, morals, and respect have always made him stand out above the crowd in a positive way.

On several occasions, I invited Marvin to speak to the youth and congregation at my church, and he always had a positive message to share with everyone. He would use himself in a humorous yet serious example to advise youth to always do their best and not make the same mistakes while they are growing up. His messages included spiritual and real-life advice needed to make everyone realize that we all have a purpose in life and that is to do all that we can in the time that we have to make this journey through life a better one for all.

I pray that God will richly bless this book so that it will bring spiritual fulfillment to everyone that Marvin could not personally meet.

Katrina A. Aikens, Teacher
Madison County Public Schools

Ms. Aikens also taught Marvin's daughter, Lyric, in second grade. And he has been the proud recipient of the "Father of the Year" award from Ms. Aikens' class.

About the Author

Marvin Terrell Mattair, AKA Merv, was born in Gainesville, Florida, and raised in Madison, Florida, where he currently lives with his wife, Denise, daughter, Lyric, and their unborn child.

His hobbies are reading, spending time with family, playing table tennis, playing flag football, working out, and helping others. He is a very strong believer in Christ, but he doesn't get caught up in the different religions.

He attended North Florida Community College for about two years, and he plans to go back and finish up his degree in the future.

Aside from working with juveniles, Marvin enjoys dejaying gospel music at weddings, receptions, and family gatherings with the assistance of Lyric & Denise. He coaches a junior football team named the Lions, and his dad is his assistant coach. He does public speaking at churches, schools, and special events. Although this is his debut book, he's currently working on another project titled, *Overcoming Seemingly Insurmountable Odds,* which will focus on how he overcame a speech impediment.

Email: Royalty@mail2.myexcel.com

Printed in the United States
200681BV00005B/307-354/A

9 780978 893774